The Dark Night Of The Soul

Lucid Poetic Noir in Twenty-One Scenes

Hannah Kreinbrink

India | USA | UK

Copyright © Hannah Kreinbrink
All Rights Reserved.

This book has been self-published with all reasonable efforts taken to make the material error-free by the author. No part of this book shall be used, reproduced in any manner whatsoever without written permission from the author, except in the case of brief quotations embodied in critical articles and reviews.

The Author of this book is solely responsible and liable for its content including but not limited to the views, representations, descriptions, statements, information, opinions, and references ["Content"]. The Content of this book shall not constitute or be construed or deemed to reflect the opinion or expression of the Publisher or Editor. Neither the Publisher nor Editor endorse or approve the Content of this book or guarantee the reliability, accuracy, or completeness of the Content published herein and do not make any representations or warranties of any kind, express or implied, including but not limited to the implied warranties of merchantability, fitness for a particular purpose.

The Publisher and Editor shall not be liable whatsoever...

Made with ♥ on the BookLeaf Publishing Platform
www.bookleafpub.in
www.bookleafpub.com

Dedication

For Connor, *mo chroí*—my eternal sunshine, my moon, and my stars whose laughter and presence remind me that time is not only an elegy, but also a hymn.

Preface

The title *The Dark Night of the Soul* borrows from St. John of the Cross, the sixteenth-century mystic who conceived of the soul's desolation as divine apprenticeship. For him, the "night" was not despair but purification—a process of unmaking in which the self is stripped of every false illumination so that the enduring may be known. I draw from this framework not as doctrine but as metaphor: an architecture of transformation that belongs as much to the psyche as to the spirit, to the modern mind as to the mystic's longing for God.

Yet the work also dwells in another lineage—the mythopoetic. Here, Olympus and Kusinara, Aphrodite and the Bodhi tree, coexist in the same breath. The Parthenon becomes a metaphor for consciousness—sacred yet weathered, eternally under restoration. These mythic allusions are not ornamental; they are instruments of scale. Through them, private experience—addiction, heartbreak, artistic awakening—attains a kind of resonance that exceeds autobiography.

Music is the other thread binding this work. Its structure is symphonic: recurring motifs of light and ruin, dissonant movements between love and renunciation, silences that speak louder than sound. Cadence becomes theology; rhythm, a form of reasoning; breath itself, a kind of prayer. Each poem is a single instrument in a larger composition—a dialogue between precision and abandon, intellect and ache.

To write in 2025 is to stand beneath a newly-forged night—one illuminated not by stars but by screens, restless and overexposed. Ours is an age of accelerated loneliness, of noise mistaken for intimacy, of data without understanding. The suffering of being human has become quieter yet more pervasive—a spiritual arrhythmia beneath the hum of progress. Still, revelation persists: in attention, in the refusal to look away, in the fragile music of persistence. To suffer consciously is to stay awake to one's own becoming—to glimpse, however briefly, the light behind the machinery.

If these poems gesture toward darkness, it is only to locate the threshold where beauty and terror converge—where one opens into the other. What emerges is not confession but anatomy: a mapping of metamorphosis in its psychological, spiritual, and aesthetic dimensions. The work carries traces of every voice, every love, disappointment, and silence that shaped it. Whatever illumination it contains is communal—borrowed from the world's passing brilliance.

Ultimately, *The Dark Night of the Soul* is not a meditation on despair but on endurance—the capacity to remain inside uncertainty long enough for it to become meaning. To undergo the night is to endure the collapse of all inherited light; to emerge from it is to recognize that illumination was never external, but latent. The light that follows does not redeem—it reveals.

Acknowledgements

This collection could not have taken shape without the people, places, and silences that insisted I keep writing through uncertainty. To my mentors and readers who saw coherence where I saw only fragments—thank you for reminding me that precision and surrender can coexist. To the friends, and my partner, Connor, who endured my late-night revisions, unspooled philosophies, and long absences - your patience is its own form of grace. To those who have suffered and kept listening for meaning - your endurance is the heartbeat of this work.

1. Where the Lovelorn Never Arrive

We were once maddened,
battle-baring in our throats—
all while we looked like an avant-garde film:
preserved, ornate, dreamlike, too.
I found they don't tolerate ambivalence here.
They're chasing sentences down caverns of meaning,
walking through tombs of memory
echoing with absence—
their absence.
There's beautiful topography
in lands away from the lovelorn.

I've seen the other side—
where silence doesn't ache but hums in a minor key,
a low-lit continuum
where the heart folds inward
like silk sinking in water.
There, love isn't performance—it's residue,
the scent of something scorched
lingering sweet in the air.
Words no longer beg to be understood;
they hang, soft-limbed and spectral,
like fog stitched across an unfamiliar sea.

I watched a figure trace alphabets in condensation—
not to be read,
but maybe just remembered.

Time stutters here.
The clocks are shy and undressed,
their hands waving like dancers
unsure if they've earned the stage.
I move swiftly along memory's fragile lattice
and choose not to climb back down.
Because it's peaceful
where the lovelorn never arrive.
Where absence is not a vacancy—
it's a room full of echoes
learning how to harmonize.

2. All Shades of Crimson Blues

Today, there is no one to keep their promise—
that last untouched desire,
the kind that holds satiation,
that brings the clapping of tongues,
now left to rot alive in its own carcass,
never to celebrate a momentary memento.

And it is only then that the fire,
that once provoked the spark dims,
bringing the last harrahs of crimson blues,
lickin' out to you under vile cackles.

Maybe I couldn't imagine—
the silence afterward,
where echoes claw their way across the walls,
where the ghost of unfinished songs
thrum like broken strings against the ribs.

All the clang and rubble, once alive,
kept in cathedrals of silence that collapse the chest—
dreams released only paper-thin, half-born,
illuminated by lanterns carried by a sunless wind.

There was no one there to keep a promise.
Not even you.

But when there is,
they're often big-bellied,
swollen from their own greed,
consuming the promises
they never meant to keep.

3. Carpe Diem

When I sleep,
Scenes flutter in the back of my eyes—
strong and realized
In the veil of slumber, I call your name.

Sometimes it was a throaty shrill, echoing to the mountains.
Sometimes, not even a murmur.
Yet always, I'd find you tangled in the cobwebs.

I think about that road less traveled,
the one we carved through dusk,
hurling a hundred miles an hour on a Harley.
My heart surged and diffused.
We were carried by the same scorched rubber.

Back then we had a streak to maintain,
riding until the sky forgot to hold its stars,
greeted by a cloud of dust that belonged to both of us.
We would catch our breath and settle in—pure,
unscathed,
with nothing else to do.

Another season,

we might plunge through the air, even faster,
yet still be carried by the same wind,
the same air that belongs to both of us.
Carrying us where we are remembered, not where we command,
leaving our fate to the natural forces that envelope us—
with nothing else to choose.

Leaving behind grandeur,
the sheer semblance, the illusion of royal status.

4. The Borrowed Transfer Ticket

He's a city slicker, a ghost of life.
He's a real harbinger, an inveigle of might.
His heavy eyelashes were always just cloaks for feelings

He smelled of elevator static and crushed mint.
Finds a way to only smile in borrowed light.
You used to finish his sentences —
now his pauses feel like locked doors.

He held your hand like a transfer ticket,
valid only for a limited time.
Once, he said your name like a secret.
Now it sounds like background noise
on a call he meant to drop.

The space beside you feels rented,
furnished with old glances and newer silences.
You could chart the drift in his coffee habits,
the way he stirs but doesn't sip.

You wonder if this is how love forgets —
not in arguments,

but in the way he doesn't look back
when he walks ahead.

5. Māyā's Dream

She dreamed in tusks of light,
a ghost-white hush entering her ribs,
heaven gesturing with an ivory trunk.
Born upright—
a boy who walked stars into the soil,
each step unfurling lotus in the four winds,
seven petals cast in cardinal grace.

Silken walls became mirrors—
they showed him everything
except the truth.
Swans bled in the garden,
stallions reared against bridled destiny.
He knew mercy before he knew fate.

Then came the sights:
time bending spines,
flesh folding in on itself,
breath leaving without ceremony—
a monk cloaked in quiet renunciation,
silence wrapped in saffron robes,
radiating what kings could not wear.

He let go of his name.

He let go of palace and past.
He sat beneath the Bodhi,
a tree older than memory,
where stillness braided itself
into thunderless light.

Not a crown,
but a great ilex writhing
like a wooden octopus,
the quiet geometry of knowing.
He spoke,
and deer turned their ears like leaves toward rain—
a sermon weaving through the groves of Sarnath.

And in the end,
beneath Sala trees in Kusinara,
he stepped not into night,
but into the space between silence and sound—
a final lotus blooming inward.

Parinirvana,
not extinguished,
but released.

6. Orchestra of War

His brand was always the rush and fervor,
iconic enough to thicken the air,
spitting venomous kerosene on the world—
a searing breath across the page of every room,
always meeting you with a brass-knuckled glimpse,
with eyes like iron hail.

Pulverized by a sound in the distance,
low and thunderous, a god's heartbeat underwater,
surrounded by nameless faces
worn into the same mask of pain.

Taut like drums stretched with grief and static—
for a moment he forgot,
but it came like a flood.
Scenes fluttered behind his eyelids,
sharp and realized, memory painted in brushstrokes:
one string tuned for every ghost.

The forty-nine strings that could be plucked
in an orchestra of ruin—
each carved from the same tree
that birthed war drums and cradles.
And every note carried the same refrain:

re-written endlessly,
the chorus of ghosts vibrating through every string.

Maybe he could name each one,
feel how each bore the marrow
of forgotten forests,
the way they could squeal out truth,
how harmony was never unity but tension,
how much pain a single string could hold
before breaking into song.

It was a spectacle—
that strings could carry a weight
that would snap even one string alone.

He thought of Mahjong:
tiles aligning by fate or strategy,
hands built slowly toward a hidden win.
Was that what this all was?
A mosaic of choices and destinies—
where some marks endure,
and others vanish in the reshuffle.

Maybe that's when he realized:
almost everyone is obsessed with leaving a mark,
bequeathing legacies
beyond the dust they become,

building scaffolds to climb out of death.

And then—
he went back to war,
silent as a cello tuning itself
before the storm.

7. The Returning Tide

On my way from the Mediterranean to Spitzberg,
I was met by white limestone cliffs—
weathered nymphs, bodies bare upon their plinths.

My hands rolling over the crests,
as if to re-sculpt the ridges,
to feel the sharpness of these bones
to feel primal again.

Then I felt it—
inside me, a returning tide.
If only I could be that fluid, that cinematic,
and so potentially harrowing.

To be—an ancient shell splayed
within the Parthenon's walls,
still singing of the sea,

Meeting the moment
when Zeus to will mortals to lose strength—
A final contact with the ocean,
the goddess Iemanjá rising—
lulled into ancient maritime currents,

a tide that does not return
but carries everything with it.

8. We Have Danced Before

I'm hesitant to lose sight of you.
I know you hang on, lurking in the faded depths
that brought you.
Because when a crescent moon looms,
there's a fervent pitch coursing through the air,
beckoning you.
A siren stitched with serpent tongues, I reckon

But it's not some highwayman or seafarer
likely to broach you uneasily.
No—just familiar eyes,
once locked with yours.
We have danced, before.

And so, I watch the moon again tonight,
wondering if it remembers our cadence—
the whispering drag of feet
against the rage of salvation.
Where your name shimmers in smoke, and temptation
wears my reflection

The jest was yours -
yet I walked away the victor.

9. Luminal Towers

I used to dream in idiosyncratic colors
luminal to those towers—
those gray rock scapes
that cry and rage against brisk foreign skies
until all that are left are booming noises laid upon echoes
of shrill,
loomed and shroud.

Oh, what wonder would point down at me
with spindly fingers,
just to leave disheveled entrails to chase.

Only from slumber can one realize dreams.
It's that hefty space between
where we proactively ensemble realities—
the place where a thousand possible fictions crowd.

Maybe a single one will billow out long enough to be
singled out,
a contour half-formed from breath and forgotten names.
Trailing the residue of what was nearly remembered,
it spins in a gravity all its own—
whispering myths in pre-verbal tongues,
each filament of thought a starless galaxy

drifting toward the architecture of intention.

In the nascent form of this dream—
between becoming and unbeing—
something rouses within the indeterminate,
where the forgotten towers now grow in the wake of shadows.

10. Before the Bread

Those clouds, billowing wonders
dispel chills with their passing—
until they welcomingly ajar,
Caught in meandering,
exchanges mere unimportant chats among themselves,
impartial to what lies below.

They watch without opinion,
and yet,
are easily moved to tears.
Dispelled by the heaviness of rain,
as if comforted in good conversation,
only to return to the earth
and be reformed again.

"Forswear all I'm born to,"
the farm will whisper then—
limbs and bones built to plough the land,
calloused like old prayers,
waiting for that long-awaited release:
to plant the wheat, heave the grain,
and make bread all over again.
"snatches of heaven", the farmer will say again

11. Ambush Behind the Screen

Eyes pour over women's bodies
like holy mountains unseen.
"Collecting experiences like relics," he'll say,
but the one he truly relishes
is the slow, curated theater of his own demise.

Oh, it's just the passer-bys—
they like to watch it burn, not shine,
to fuel the latest fad that caught flame.
They'll swipe up, down, right, left, and all around—
delivering verdicts in a blink,
casually cruel and unwelcomingly quaint,
 intimacy the raffle, and attention the consolation prize.

The arrows of vanity, unfortunately, go both ways,
 hoping to rise above the limericks presented today.
These are narrow universes we've indulgently seen—
a quick buck paid for conspirators in mischief,
and for fifteen minutes of fame.

12. Silence of the Ram

I collect bruises from silence—
languid blinks from the icy eyes of the Ram.
I never thought he'd watch so quietly,
for such an eternity,
all while I sit in my own wretchedness,
perhaps waiting for a swift ego death.
Sleeping and moping through his shallow draughts,
hoping for one true drink
from his Pierian spring.

I've always been Earth,
rooted by the constellations—
patient beneath Saturn's slow-turning eye.
But the Ram is the Cardinal Flame—
born of fire and motion,
crashing into and out of my orbit,
bringing hell to the ground while I spun out of rotation.
Still, all is fair in love and war.

At some point, I begged you to witness my life—
burned in memory, the antithesis of a love letter,
perfectly folded on your bedside.
Met only by a little grimace,
like the last sacrament before embalming.

Asheville's season turned,
the backdrop outgrew our story:
pollen and manure
thickened the breath of Blue Ridge mist.
You're leaving in time for Christmas,
and heading west.

The last message
lodged itself like daggers
between the vertebrae of my spine—
and stayed there far too long.
Left to writhe in my own wrath of unprocessed emotion,
I learn to find ground, and from the ashes,
to be Earth again.

13. St. Edmund

St. Edmund wasn't named after a saint;
he was named after an island—
a man of a thousand faces,
each wearing sunken sockets to hold bewildered eyes.
Perhaps that's why there was always a map
flapping wildly in his hands,
or clenched between his teeth.

They said his presence was a glitch beneath a searing siege.
I only hoped to be shipped to one of his islands,
in the span of my time.

There were days when sunlight would pervade the panels after dawn,
when music would fill the room—
he was playing *Clair de Lune.*
When he'd release his final note, I began to search,
trying to find his sharp blue eyes,
the ones that dulled to vapor when he looked away.

Or I'd study his veins—
those twisted interstates
carrying blood to the locus of my questions:

a heart I never knew.

All the while,
my interest slipped away from the wider world.
I was mystified,
bewitched by the shapeliness and tweedy splinters of truth
that could shred someone to bits
just in time for rationality to barge on through.

To let love's pride drift into the big-bellied wider world
with no avail,
to realize I was only a dreary moon—Earth's mad companion.
There'd be that showy bravado moment when I'd fall out of orbit—
with a whimper, a gasp, and finally a sigh—
to graduate into being real: wild and wide-eyed.

14. Response to Desiderata

We could play the history of your vinyl skin,
once dazzled with iridescence—
pack you off with a round of applause
and tie off your sweeter amendments
until the next passenger bursts into your freshly minted,
gleaming reverie.
While the waves of this ocean we hold steady,
shushing the gentle whisper of the trees.

Before drifting away through bountiful space and time,
day by day, the moon and stars buoying up,
as if carried by grand balloons of escape—
then to be sunk down in troughs of color,
as if strung out of every bit of life.
At just the turn of a cheek,
when you once felt that side of your face flush
from the heat of concentration,
but only you could blush a deeper crimson
by the same stroke of good fortune.

You'd watch a stranger with a pocket watch
pass without a moment's recognition,
leaving behind the scent of sweat and crushed roses,
of gardenia and sandalwood.

Deeper than the blood that exalts
piety and justice,
the smell of life and its renditions
permeates between thick spines,
to be passed onto your kin.
A new eye shelters focus now,
pressed lips harboring a secret
your bones and limbs once ached to know.

Leaving behind the grandeur of royal status
for a life unknown—
to rest at last,
as a secret triumph.

15. Young Hunter's Errand

This is the kind of day
that makes me want to frolic—
half-mad in a gaudy leotard,
somewhere drenched by the sun, unmarred,
in a country I can't pronounce.
And that's what we did.

We descended through Bourges, into the beauty of holiness,
pink and bronze skin glinting against the jade hush of foliage.
Then something winged—the torchbearer of folly—
caught us.
I bet when the son of Mercury, that cherubic archer, saw us,
his unweaned lips were singing softly the songs of unsung heroes.

He trembled. It was his youngest arrow trembling—
the good old hunter's quiver:
one gold-tipped, one lead-tipped,
hesitant,
yet somehow making the moment feel immense.
He aimed from above, foie gras on his fingers,

and an arrow sang through the air
like a thread of honeyed light.

It dawned on us, rather irrefutably,
caught in the frenzy of insatiability,
to quickly learn the frivolity of the heart.
And it came in sheer semblance—
met by caramel, gold pools of eyes,
a bray of laughter,
and something vast and unseen
unfolding between two souls
in pursuit of the same fool's errand.

That's when I noticed his veins,
overflowing on your skin like rivers on an antique map.
I knew his prayers were cut thin,
at least for today.
Omnia vincit amor—
but I will live just to see where they end.

16. End the Farce

I promised to stay where the soil knows my name.
You told me to take root and let the earth do its work.
In this season,
my tree's brittle leaves carry the promise of autumn,
still reaching, even as the light recedes.

But when I'm six feet under,
something restless stirs—
the kind of panic that blooms where the heart should rest,
seeping through the roots,
finding every hollow it can fill,
until vacancy makes its home.

Folded back into the greater pulse of the Earth,
more impenetrable than night itself,
where stillness hums where breath once was,
and the dark learns my name—
and the farce of living, at last, ends.

17. Lurid Haze

The static gets deafening
when thoughts become a frenzy of insatiability.
It becomes a mission to catch lightning in a jar—
a swig of brandy felt ideal,
a quick way to turn a raw evening
into a spectacle.

They will watch from afar,
by two or three—
the sweet, heavy-tongued, relishing connoisseur
thinks otherwise.

In this lurid haze,
I find myself tracing crowns of cigarettes
and feeling pulses like waves of silhouettes.
Now, happily a mere unentity,
balancing on the knife-edge
of this thirst's ache.

Hope De Jour

When did I find this new reservoir?
I've only ever felt like I made the Sun drop dead—
spent afternoons tracing infinite lines between my head,
only to fall asleep in strange places,
feeling loosely held, met by tight gazes.

There's a self-parodying wit to it:
how does one allocate *healthy grievances*?
Owing to their permanence—
along with taxes and all—*ha.*

Do all my words get lain between my thick spine,
waiting to be passed onto my kin?
While I squander the currency of time,
pillaging the architecture of meaning.

And if they find these pages someday,
will they mistake my restlessness for wisdom?
Or see it plain—
a body trying to rewrite its bloodline,
trading faith for syntax,
silence for a name.

Still, I leave the lines open-ended,

hoping they'll be filled better than I could.
I'll keep asking, if only to hear who answers.
For thou art governed by nature—
and I, by the need to create.
to infuse light again into each morning—
my own small *hope de jour.*

19. Cheap, Situated Infatuation

There was a time you'd hold my face in your hands
like you were relentless to shatter glass—
dizzied, spinning out of your embrace.
Then you'd realize this and tower over me,
tall and gaunt,
the percussion of your body,
particularly the rhythm of your skin,
roused every pore of my sweltering whims.

Crumbling brownstones and row houses—
we'd head downtown for neon nuances
and your pickpockets.

We talked about leaving north;
it was the fashion of a new time and place.
But you left without me—
not even a far-sighted reflection of you
left for me to retrace.

Still, I wear your shirts to get closer to the fragrance
of sunshine, Marlboros,
and cheap, situated infatuation.

The sequel wasn't a sequel—
it was a prelude.

I drew hard on a cigarette
until the ember mirrored the Sun,
and the smoke split the air
Like two ghosts dissolving into dawn

20. Maverick of the Freaks

They file in neat rows, maybe by the dozen—
cookie-cutter humans,
cocked heads and inquisitive glances,
always met by unsmiling earnestness.
Cue the fluorescence,
And the sterile hymn of sameness.

They are the resin flowers
that only bloom beneath apothecary light,
kept captive—
half-alive, curious things,
never of scent,
never decaying quite the same way.

Hide the Maverick in the covers
of marbled serenity,
where the perfume of burnt potpourri
haunts the air like memory.

They are a hymn gone feral.
They will rage against the squabble of power,
the whisper of forbidden literature,
where one dares to become
the misfit's requiem—

a tender war cry against monotony.

Lurch with an off-rhythm heartbeat,
Where they can laugh loud enough
to crack the porcelain hush.

For all that is strange is holy,
and all that is holy
was once set to flame
for being strange.

21. The Dawn After

First, the light left.
Not in anger,
but as an apprenticeship through divine withdrawal.

One is presented with an ongoing, active choice—
to enter your own metamorphosis
or, alternatively,
to be indispensable and forcibly shaped.

Without it, we would be amorphous
and rigid, assorted contusions
pressed against our own perceived limits.

Life, that grande vaudeville of charades and conundrums —
the vulgar jokes and meandering stories —
is only a choreography of illusion.

Yet, trussed and caged is never a place to be.
One could plunge through the aperture,
to rage against it if you must
until the dark unthreads itself—
to face the light of a differentiated salvation,
we can then no longer be frightened into stillness.

Now the light does not blind—
it glints across what remains of you,
unornamented, bare,
and still—
you bow to it,
you let it in.

After night, there is no fanfare,
no revelation,
only the quiet arrival of a self that no longer hides—
to wake up to a new Earth, riveting and beckoning you in,
emptied enough to hold up the whole sky.

www.ingramcontent.com/pod-product-compliance
Lightning Source LLC
Chambersburg PA
CBHW070039070426
42449CB00012BA/3103